Poetry Idol

Everlasting Ink

Edited By Sarah Washer

First published in Great Britain in 2018 by:

Young Writers
Remus House
Coltsfoot Drive
Peterborough
PE2 9BF
Telephone: 01733 890066
Website: www.youngwriters.co.uk

All Rights Reserved
Book Design by Ashley Janson
© Copyright Contributors 2017
SB ISBN 978-1-78820-335-7
Printed and bound in the UK by BookPrintingUK
Website: www.bookprintinguk.com
YB0341L

Foreword

Dear Reader,

Welcome to *Poetry Idol – Everlasting Ink*.

This wonderful collection of poetry focuses on the people that these young poets look up to. Using a mix of imagination, expression and poetic styles, this anthology is an impressive snapshot of the inventive, original and skilful writing of young people today, expressing their appreciation for the people, and things, that mean the most to them.

Young Writers was established in 1991 to nurture creativity in our children and young adults, to give them an interest in poetry and an outlet to express themselves. Seeing their work in print will encourage them to keep writing as they grow and become our poets of tomorrow.

Selecting the poems has been challenging and immensely rewarding. The effort and imagination invested by these young writers makes their poems a pleasure to enjoy reading time and time again. It also made picking a winner a very difficult task, so well done to *Huzaifa Ali* who has won a selection of books and a hamper!

Sarah Washer

Contents

Winner:

Huzaifa Ali (9) — 1

Independent Entries

Ethan-Raul Patel — 3
Arjav Poudel (14) — 4
Faith Toluwanimi Eleduma (12) — 7
Jennifer Mery Howitt — 8
Jayavarshini Sankaran (13) — 11
Reanna Valerie Denson-Smith (13) — 12
Jamie Cavallo (16) — 14
Lauren Clair Jackson (12) — 16
Chloe Richardson (15) — 19
Sarann Kinsey John (13) — 20
Isobel Wilson (12) — 22
Saarah Ahmed (17) — 24
Sumbal Arshad (15) — 26
Eva Skye Reid-Gordon (10) — 28
Taslima Khanom (13) — 30
Ella-Rose Mulcare — 32
Christopher Chiocca (16) — 34
Katie Graden — 36
Jessica Ella Stephens (9) — 38
Jack Lee (8) — 40
Aleema Mirza Hamid (11) — 42
Hafsah Saleem (11) — 44
Megan Amelia Eastwood (14) — 46
David Aderibigbe — 48
Tinotenda Tekenende (12) — 50
Anya Main (10) — 52
Natalie Ann Hughes (18) — 54
Karla Elaine Shuttlewood (11) — 56
Benjamin Adam Wright — 58

Ewan Austin (17) — 60
Fereshta Amiri (17) — 62
Halima Bahnan (13) — 64
Isabelle Kimberley — 66
Asvitha Sarma (11) — 68
Emma Cartwright (11) — 70
Harrison Taylor Commons (15) — 72
Imogen Searles (7) — 74
Aaria Bains (6) — 76
Sarah Manning (11) — 77
Georgia Clarice Paxton-Doggett (17) — 78
Ayesh Mohsin — 80
Dami Daniel Olawoye (13) — 81
Kiera Douglas — 82
Sophie Lucketti (10) — 84
Kethusha Saseestharan (13) — 85
Laurel Smith (13) — 86
Tasnim Adan (11) — 88
Somi Angel Ramona Ejiro Enaife (11) — 90
Esther Kaombe Ngwewa (9) — 91
Jessica Downe (14) — 92
Hollie Mae Tapper (15) — 93
Udit Mahalingam — 94
Mariam Khan (12) — 95
Katie Stewart (18) — 96
Sophie Louise Evans (14) — 97
Rahul Vijay Singh (9) — 98
Maria Manta (12) — 99
Alaha Baig (11) — 100
Zoe Lewis (9) — 101
Rishika Singh (14) — 102
Bareerah Chughtai (13) — 103
Amalia Maria Mitrovici (12) — 104
Monica Mustapha — 105

Josh Takhi (13)	106
Priya Vijay Singh (14)	107
Vedika Hemanth Gowda (11)	108
Joshua Wagner (9)	109
Alice Burns (11)	110
Sineidin Serlom Tamakloe	111
Rithika Raghunandanan (8)	112
Hope Stokes (11)	113
Derin Ester Iyapo (10)	114
Freya Anderson (8)	115
Samuel Osborn (9)	116
Eliza Shearn (7)	117
Freya Butler (13)	118
Sehrish Malik	119
Ryan King	120
Benjamin Robert Francis Fletcher (13)	121
Armaan Mohammed (14)	122
Sophie Parsons (9)	123
Maddie Bradfield (9)	124
Courtney Harney	125
Nina Holguin	126
Karen Kou (10)	127
Leah Young (11)	128
Lucyanne Reid (16)	129
Molly Emery (16)	130
Joanna Ezeonu (9)	131

Cranbourne Primary School, Winkfield

Danai Symona Mushambi (10)	132
Flo Taylor (10)	134
Lauren Ellis (9)	136
Amrita Charan Evans (9)	138
Evelyn Fraser (10)	139
Harry Graham Dommett (11)	140
Isabelle Perkins (10)	142
Ellie Wishart-Core (9)	144
Logan Horsley (10)	146
Mikey Verga (10)	147
Hunnie Louise Crump (10)	148
Poppy Alice Jackson (10)	150
Ollie Riley (10)	152

Max Roy Cantrell-Bennett (10)	153
Thomas Atack (10)	154
George Jones (11)	155

Eastwood High School, Newton Mearns

Katie Grant	156

Hampton College, Hampton Vale

Renai Bennett (12)	157
Toni Carla Van Wyk (12)	158
Isabel Olivia Grainger (12)	160

Mayfair International Academy, Estepona

Elias Holm Johansen (9)	161
Alfie Irvine (9)	162
Suraj Robson Singh	163

The Compass Primary Academy, Kettering

Bethany Halls (9)	164
Matthew Ellis (9)	165
Gvidas Jakutavicius (10)	166
Olivia Whitney (8)	167
Hannah Marindire (10)	168
Paige Brennan (8)	169
Theo Reed (8)	170
Princess Rhiannon Bowes (9)	171
Logan John Cross (9)	172
Ruby Sabrina Birkett (8)	173
Charlie Frost (8)	174
Simrah Kaur	175
Tyler Bugg (8)	176
Ali Abdullah (10)	177
Aaliyah Melton (9)	178

The Poems

My Special Someone

There is a special someone in my life,
Who is not like me or you.
He is special in a special kind of way,
And he just wants to be accepted too.

My significant special someone,
Is the kindest person I know.
He would not harm a fly,
But recently he's been feeling low.

This is why I have decided
To dedicate this poem to him
Because he tries to remove all my problems
Even though he is full to the brim.

My outstanding special someone,
Always gets into trouble just for me.
He will pretend that it was his fault

And he will never charge a fee.

Because to him love is free
It does not cost any money.
He is a listening ear and a helping hand,
Be it rainy or sunny.

My important special someone,
Is unique in a unique kind of way.
He has a disability you see,
A disability that's here to stay.

But that's not a bad thing I tell you,
It makes him different and like no other
My special someone is...
My amazing big brother!

Huzaifa Ali (9)

What Is A Mum?

A weaner and musher, a milky tooth-brusher
A rocker and feeder, a storytime-reader
A fairy cake-baker and fancy dress-maker
A wiper and washer, and bad habit-squasher
A dirty sheet-changer, a room re-arranger
A keen stain-remover, a wielder of Hoover
A peeler and cooker, appointment-booker
A loyal defender and Christmas card-sender
A playdate-arranger, alerter of danger
A suitcase-packer, a dishwasher-stacker
A 'be quiet' hisser, a cuddly kisser
An early riser, a birthday-surpriser
A list-compiler, a proud parent smiler
A talented wrapper, a tireless clapper
A lavatory-flusher, a praiser and gusher
A listening ear, a good refereer
A source of a fiver, a free taxi driver
A smoothie-blender and broken heart-mender
A consummate shopper, embarrassing bopper
A grocery bagger and homework nagger
That's what makes a mum!

Ethan-Raul Patel

Eternal Father

Ever since I was little, I was always asking questions
Sometimes important, albeit the babbling of an attention-seeking toddler
I would always have something or another to test you on
And you would always have the best answer ready

Through your words I felt consoled, a deeper understanding
And the wisdom of a man whose voice
alone inspired me to push myself
Further than I ever could
The determination and the struggle to live up to your name, let alone surpass it

Meandering down the winding roads, the single objective of earning your pride, following footsteps of the greatest father there ever was, or will be
We've had our quarrels; our beliefs have often parted ways
But you serve as the tide that ensures my boat never ever goes astray

In a sea of ideals, it's easy to get lost
Searching, in the quest for the perfect, textbook father
Fortunately though, I don't have to look quite so far
To see the man who strives tirelessly, for the benefit of his loved ones

As a doctor, you help; you heal and save the lives of those that need you
And at the end of the day, the work comes home
You help them, you heal us, you save me every day
And I don't care for the neurological diseases, or nights in an under-staffed ward

I look up to you, more than anyone else
For many more reasons than anyone else
Because I've had more experience than anyone else
Of the virtues that set you apart, from everyone else

As a son, I hope I will have made you the proudest you have ever been
The oceans may bleed dry, but even then I won't be led astray

Because I will have the ever-faithful tide, you at my side
Guiding me, all the way

And I'll know if I too, become a good man
When I have wonderful children, the spitting image of me
And this time, I'll be the one guiding them, through the stormy waters ahead
Helping, healing and saving lives

As my idol watches and smiles, remembering a little boy, with a lot of questions
The most demanding patient ever to grace his office, his home, his life
But how the times will change one day, the patient will be long gone
Up and over boyhood, straight out and through the gate

You will be my patient then, and I'll be serving you
You are my patient, dad...
Patience, love doesn't wait.

Arjav Poudel (14)

The Importance Of School

My mum she's supported and laboured for me
She's shown how important education can be
At age three she left her house
To live with her auntie and her spouse
as she got older she wanted to leave
And go to uni just like her friends
But her dad said no 'cause of what he believed
that why should he spend so much money
on a woman who will grow to get married?
He said there's no point, he ruined her dreams
that's why my mum supports us by all means
A few years later my mum met my dad
They got married, had us then moved to England
My dad had a job so quickly, so fast
But my mum, she wasn't working and a few years had passed
She couldn't get a job she liked, you see
'Cause there weren't many options for her to be
But my mum will always tell me not to be like her
Rather to focus more at school and be the best I can.

Faith Toluwanimi Eleduma (12)

In My Mother's Bedroom

My mother was the moon;
after night-long nightmares
she cocooned me in her arms,
her warm hugs thawed the darkness.

She held me there,
on the mint-blue duvet,
with neutral walls like sand dunes,
pristine sheets wrinkled with laughter
from the claw that came down, the tickle monster.
It was there
with hair that shone bronze like a two pence coin,
my mother told me stories of dragons
and Greek philosophers
her voice calm like an ocean breeze.

That bed,
sandwiched between two sets of drawers,
the nick-nacks had been swept inside,
concealed
and the floor, white carpet, stainless steel.

My mother wore jeans
but her wardrobe was lined with suits
gathering dust.

The greatest mystery was the dirty linen basket,
cankered willow twisted in rippled wood
forming a wall inside of which lay
her darkest secrets. When I gazed
into her eyes, a twinkle
a hidden dirty sock

When I heard the diagnosis I didn't cry at first,
I sat on the stairs, staring at the books about dragons,
looking across at this door, this barrier.

She just lay there,
under the mint-blue duvet,
the blinds leaking dripping sunlight
yet the room was darkness,
the walls, the night,
and the bed and the white floor were
shadows.

I knocked on this door,
there she stood, head scarf exposed. But
the light shone on the dirty linen basket,
toppled over, clothes
so dirty oozing out
of the willow prison.

In my new house, my mother's bedroom
had three neutral sandy walls,
a mint-blue duvet, and a shield of glass,
light dry dust, filling all the drawers of nick-nacks.
When I gazed into her eyes
a veil had been lifted;
I could hear her heartbeat.

Jennifer Mery Howitt

Poonam Raut, The Inspirational Indian Woman Cricketer

P oonam Raut, the one who made my dreams shimmer.
O n the day I saw her play, she instantly took over my dreams.
O h how she swings her bat, sending the ball miles away so that you can't see where it went.
N ever has she given up on playing cricket.
A t times, she fails on her batting, but has that ever stopped her from playing?
M any fans she has gained and in return she gave us dreams.

R unning, batting, bowling and fielding, how many more skills does she know?
A ll the time, she is improving more and more but is there a limit for her improvement.
U nder, over, sideways and up, in all directions, her balls go around.
T ime flies by, like the balls she sends flying high, but will my dreams fly high?

Jayavarshini Sankaran (13)

You Were There Since Day One

A strong warrior, not disappointing
Straight into action, no need for loitering

Reliable, responsible and reassuring
With them around no danger is lurking

If I will grow up to be anything like them I will do myself proud,
I can spot them from miles off, even in a crowd

They comfort us in every single way
Walked with us every single day

Supporting me with all my decisions and actions
Helping me with the hard things
Like life skills, and little things such as fractions

I fall, I fail, I break down and cry
You pick me up and help me to fly

You were there for me since day one
I will be there for you until our days are done

Until death we part
You will still be in our hearts

D for dearly loved
A for always there for me
D for deserving all the things you desire
D for dedicating your heart and soul to your family
Y for you, because you are my hero, my inspiration!

This project is to write about your hero, in fact a poem
So I thought I would tell them...

About my rock, my world, my moon and my stars,
Without you I wouldn't know where to start
You love your children equally,
but your little girl has a special place in your heart

'She's a daddy's girl,' everyone will mention
I'm too busy looking for you, not listening or paying attention

Dear fathers everywhere, we love you!
But mine is the best, happy birthday Dad!

Reanna Valerie Denson-Smith (13)

My Idol - Agatha Christie

A gatha Christie is the idol of my life,
G etting me through all my troubles, pains and strife,
A shocking ending in Christie's work was rife.
T here are so many reasons as to why she shouldn't be defamed,
H er way of showing betrayal and who really should be blamed,
A nd all because true love has sparked and glowed and flamed.

C an we take a minute to take in her sheer skill?
H ow she makes so many stories, just based around free will,
R eading every line to find out who is next to kill.
I 'm going to throw it out there; she simply is the best,
S he's inventive and she's witty and to me there is no contest,
T he crown goes out to Agatha, there, the winner has been addressed.

I t's the way she made so many new whodunnits,
E ven how she could make you cry and leave your heart in bits,
S howcasing her brains, her emotions and her wits.

A lso, her work shows what talent she truly had
'B ig Four', 'Third Girl' and 'They came from Baghdad'
'C at among the pigeons' is just a further one to add.

M arple and Poirot always help to hasten a case,
U tilising every emotion that a person can embrace,
R ightly so, her books lay proud upon my bookcase.
D eservedly so, I think it must be said, because
E ach and every chapter is so meticulously sculpted.
R eading every line as perfectly as she orders. Like how mine
S pell out the words 'Agatha Christie's ABC Murders'.

Jamie Cavallo (16)

My Heroine

After much deliberation and thought
Process done, my mind is made up.
My heroine's my mum
And she's proven to me,
Time after time and I have laid it out for you,
In this Easter time rhyme.

My mum's 37, 5 foot odd,
With black hair,
She uses dye to hide the fact
From the world she is grey.
She is loud,
You can hear her down the street
When she talks
And she's eight months pregnant
And hobbles when she walks.
She is really chatty,
Even talks in her sleep
And once she gets started
She could talk a glass eye to sleep.

But when it's her turn to listen,
Her sense of hearing has left,
You could be sat right beside her
And she's suddenly deaf.

She's on Facebook a lot,
I say it's bad for her health,
And she thinks she is funny,
Which is funny itself,
And she also likes singing
When no one is around,
I bet the neighbours both sides
Think a cat is being drowned.

But all jokes aside
My mum is the best,
She's kind and she's thoughtful,
Hardly ever gets stressed.
She's loving, she's pretty,
She has a beautiful smile,
Even though she does a loud fart
Every once in a while!

You think this poem's not Eastery,
Well your pardon I beg,
Like I said, she's pregnant!
So she is shaped like an egg!

Lauren Clair Jackson (12)

My Friend, My Neighbour, My Idol

She walked a dark, lonely path that one day, many of us may brace,
Yet as she did, unafraid and unknowing, a smile still graced her face.
She remained strong, while those around her crumbled and cried,
She remained calm and took every little thing in her stride.
At night, I wished, hoped I could take her pain away,
But soon it seemed that cancer was there to stay.
She came home and we were relieved, thankful, glad,
She went back and we were devastated, hurt, sad.
But as she walked that dark, lonely path of pain,
Where a breeze turned to wind and the sun to rain.
Still she smiled and held her head up high,
While it was us around her, who dared to cry.
She was brave without realizing, sick without complaining, a hero without trying,
And if I were to say that I don't love and idolize her, my dear, I would be lying.

Chloe Richardson (15)

A Welsh Warrior Princess

She is known by many, in the history books she lays,
She fought for her country but there was a price to pay.
Without waiting for anyone, she prepared to fight,
They journeyed over mountains day and night.
She was just a Welsh princess but she did not hesitate,
With Maurice De Londres on his way, they couldn't just wait.
With her two sons and farmers she led Wales to battle,
Quietly they travelled without so much as a prattle.
A Welsh man betrayed them and exposed their plan,
The enemy approached so the army ran,
Like Judas Iscariot and his thirty silver coins,
He betrayed his own kinsmen with the men he did join.
Swords started clashing and the war began,
Men started dying from each clan.

The leadership she showed was courageous as anyone had seen
And the courage she showed was simple, supreme.
Her son's life was taken but she continued to fight,
With sorrow and a heavy heart she showed great might.
The crusade carried on but they began to fall,
But the inspiring princess continued to brawl.
The battle went downhill and they were sadly beat,
The enemy brought her and her last son with them before they could retreat,
They showed no mercy to young lady and boy,
The invaders looked only to mutilate and destroy.
The cruel rivals slayed the mother in front of her son,
Before taking his young life by the body of his mum.
We will never forget her incredulous sacrifice,
Gwenllian, the Princess of Wales, we will always remember her heroic, valiant life.

Sarann Kinsey John (13)

Olivia

She's short but sweet and cute in every single way possible,
She can be annoying but barely ever!
She's caring and is always there for when you need reassurance
She supports you with every decision you make,
Never going against you.

I once went to a theme park with her
We had a load of fun
We ate chicken burgers and stuffed our mouths with candyfloss
We screamed blue murder on roller coasters
We slept at my house, and watched Netflix all night long.

We once went shopping, to every trendy shop
In New Look and Topshop, and everything else you can imagine a girl in,
We bought matching outfits,
We had KFC and gossiped about our friends.
We slept in my living room, and watched chick flicks like Mean Girls.

One day at school we thought we were from Pretty Little Liars
Acting like spies and trying to figure out everyone's secrets
We never did. But we had fun trying.

But someone got in-between us for a month.
She manipulated her into not liking me.
But she figured it out and came back to me,
It was just us for ages.

We now involve everyone
And notice when someone tries to split us up
And we always dodge those people.
This is my best friend, she's called Olivia or Liv or Olive
You can call her Ollie,
But in my case she's my favourite person.

Isobel Wilson (12)

My Mother Is My Idol In Every Form

It is true that there is a God but he is unknown.
I see the form of God in my mother, in every form.
The land we live on is my mother.
A mother is a safeguard, she protects her children with shelter.

A mother gives us life, hope, will and determination.
She holds our hands to teach us how to work.
We see the world sitting on her shoulder.
My mother is in the form of God
Though it is true that there is a God but he is unknown.

A mother teaches us how to distinguish between right and wrong.
How does one account for all we're blessed?
It's not easy to describe the word mother and her role.
The universe needs a mother, a child needs a mother for their survival.

Lord is recognised on Earth and everywhere,
Yet we can see Lord in the form of our mother.
Though it is true that there is a God but he is unknown.

A mother is seen everywhere.
A mother gives us birth, her children are her life.
A mother stays up at night.
A mother has lullabies on her lips and her eyes spin with dreams for us.
A mother sacrifices her sleep for us,
Bears all sorrows with a smile.
A mother is a blessing for her children in the form of the Lord.
Though it is true there is a god but he is unknown.

Saarah Ahmed (17)

Malala, You Are My Idol

Malala Yousafzai is her name,
From one bullet she was nearly left insane.

Gratefully, she managed to survive,
The Taliban were left surprised.

Toor Pekai is her mother's name,
Always wants her daughter to be at top grade.

When she heard that Malala had been shot,
She didn't know where to plot.

Quickly, Malala and family moved countries,
Moved to a new place for lots to see.

Malala still carried on with her education,
6 A*s and 4 As in her GCSE examination.

3 As in A-levels achieved by her,
To step into education even further.

Was stepping up for education Malala's mistake?
That she had to leave her country to stay safe.

She wants to go back,
But right now there's lots to pack.

She loves to read and write,
And stepping up for education was her right.

She is still carrying on with her studies,
In Oxford, one of the best Universities.

And she deserves it,
Because not even a bullet can affect who she is.

I am so proud a girl like her exist,
Because without her, there wouldn't had been a fix

Malala you are my idol,
And you always will be for many girls around the world.

Sumbal Arshad (15)

Who Do I Idolise?

I idolise J K Rowling, she inspires me.
Why?
She's won multiple awards.
She's a best-selling author.
She's an OBE.
She's a screenwriter.
She's a film producer.
She wrote the best
And favourite series (Harry Potter).
She has inspirational quotes that inspire me.
You sort of start thinking anything's possible
If you've got enough nerve
To the well-organised mind,
Death is but the next great adventure.
Youth cannot know how age thinks and feels.
But old men are guilty
If they forget what it was to be young.
I want to become a writer one day.
I'll write about my adventure
With someone special.

I idolise many other people
Including Jamie Oliver and David Walliams.
I chose J K Rowling especially
Because of all her success in life.
I'm ten.
My only real success
Is to be a published author in three books.
She is just... I can't even describe
How much she inspires me.
She's written astonishingly
Bewildering books like Harry Potter.
Her books just keep coming,
I'm excited to see if she writes
Another fantasy series -
It wouldn't be surprising if she did.

Eva Skye Reid-Gordon (10)

My Idol

Many choose to idolise the perfect,
Or the pretty,
While others choose the direct,
Or the witty.
But I'm not many or others,
As I idolise the bullied, and the disabled,
Who show no covers.
Those amazing people out there
Who put up with so much,
Yet won't break with simply a touch.
Those who no longer know the meaning of life,
But always takes the other option
Instead of the knife,
Because it's all these people
That make the world go around,
That make us realise
That not everything's sweet and sound.
I salute those out there who carry on going,
Even though it feels like they're just lowering.
Soon, they'll be up there glowing in the light,
And it's all just 'cause they didn't lose this fight.

All of you who pity these lot,
Will all be in for quite a shock.
When you see their capabilities,
You'll be here, with no future possibilities.
So next time you see the bullied or disabled,
Remember they're my idols,
And help show them they're enabled,
To be given a chance at life,
Because it's their human right.

Taslima Khanom (13)

My Idol

Sometimes I sit and wonder what it would be like to be my idol,
She sits tight in the family bridle.
We are her horses and she is our mare,
Without her, love would be lost and life unfair.
Passionate about my future she dreams about my job, my career,
And although we argue, I couldn't imagine her not being here.
Yes that's right, you know who you are,
You're my mother, my friend, my bright shining star.
And if things turn sour,
She's here to save the hour.
She's the boss and don't forget it,
But her smile is like a bulb being lit.
And every night she comes to wish me well,
We tell each other secrets, but she promises never to tell.
She's a legend in our household,
No one could take her place even when she's dying and old.

Words cannot describe how much fun we have together,
But you'd better remember she's my mum and she's got my back forever.
And I have hers too,
Because Mummy, I love you.
She lights up a room when she walks in,
Her beautiful voice has no sins.
She's got the halo of an angel and kindness of a butterfly,
But one day when she's gone I will whisper to you that our love never did die.

Ella-Rose Mulcare

Einaudi, Classical Extraordinaire

L isten to the way he plays the piano,
U niting his listeners with a blissful melody.
D evoting all my time to learn his compositions is
O ne thing I love to do,
V olume to the maximum as
I play the beautiful tune.
C lassical music is extremely underrated,
O n a teenager's phone at least.

E veryone I know listens to songs with
I dentical beats and chords.
N ot that they'd understand this -
A fter all, they do not appreciate
U nique and original pieces.
D o you even know who this is about?
I 'm talking about Ludovico Einaudi, of course!

I nspiration in the form of a person,
N o better way to describe him,
S ince he inspired me to play the
P iano as beautifully as he does.
I cannot understand why classical music is

R ejected in today's society, as
E very piece and composition can
S park inspiration in every person who listens.

M y inspiration to play piano professionally is
E inaudi, a classical extraordinaire.

Christopher Chiocca (16)

The One And Only Pastor Natalie

Inspiring, motivating and encouraging;
Natalie makes a difference,
Changes lives and makes this world a better place.
Compassionate, kind-hearted and selfless;
She copes with almost unbearable pressure to help
People;
She is uplifting,
Even when life is being so unbelievably
Challenging.
Natalie never stops believing in you;
Even when you don't believe in yourself.
Easy to talk to and forever willing to give up her
Time;
She is with you always and not just through good
Times.
God's word is alive in her heart and it shows in her
Work and life;
She teaches you to be content, compassionate and
Caring.

Her dedication, commitment and hard work is
Phenomenal.
Without her, I wouldn't be where I am today;
I would still be lost, broken and unsatisfied.
She has shown me that nothing shall be
Impossible,
For His kingdom reigns unstoppable.
She helps me to stay strong,
And use life's challenges to grow stronger in my
Faith.
She is a role model, a great leader and an amazing
Friend.
God has truly blessed the world.

Katie Graden

Dance Inspiration

The lights go out
And the audience settle
The dancers are preparing themselves
Being quiet and still just like a petal

Then the curtain rises
And the music begins
They leap onto the stage
As though they had wings

Delicate and dainty
With pointed toes
Making works of art
With every beautiful pose

My heart skips a beat
With every plie
As the dancers lift their feet
With every petit jete

A pair of dancers
Do their duet

They leap from each side
And perform a perfect pirouette

The audience smile
And begin their applause
I nearly cry
This is all because

The girls on stage are truly amazing
To me they're the best,
They are my inspiration
Thanks to the dance teacher
This dance school is the best location

These girls are my friends
Who I really do love
They are like angels
From up above.

Jessica Ella Stephens (9)

What Shall We Do With The Grumpy Teacher?

What shall we do with the grumpy teacher?
What shall we do with the grumpy teacher?
Early in the morning.

Hang her from a wooden climbing frame,
Call her a very nasty name.
Don't let her catch you pulling faces,
Put work back in the correct places.
Early in the morning.

Ooh ray and up she rises,
Ooh ray and up she rises,
Early in the morning.

What shall we do with the grumpy teacher?
What shall we do with the grumpy teacher?
Early in the morning.

Put her stinky clothes inside out,
So that she looks like a smelly snout.

Paint her face like an evil witch,
Feed her a wiggly worm sandwich
Early in the morning.

Ooh ray and up she rises,
Ooh ray and up she rises,
Early in the morning.

What shall we do with the grumpy teacher?
What shall we do with the grumpy teacher?
Early in the morning.

Rotate her like a never-stopping fidget spinner,
Make a plateful of baked beans for dinner.
She wishes to find her very best mate,
Early in the morning.

Jack Lee (8)

My Poetry Idol

My mum is my idol,
My favourite person in the universe!
Why?
She makes my heart burst.

She never gives up,
Always pushes herself higher than the limit.
When she enters the room,
She makes me smile in a minute.

Doesn't care about what people think,
Tries harder and harder like a lion searching for his prey.
She always makes sure I have enough food,
She would bring dinner to me on a tray.

She likes to have fun!
(Me too!)
I'll be hiding in the cupboard,
Until she comes and shouts, 'Boo!'

She takes risks,
And will do anything for me.

I'm always wanting to explore here,
There and everywhere,
She thinks I'm her busy bee.

My mum is the world to me!
I love my mother!
I mean the world to her,
All she likes to do is smother!

That's my idol, my mother!

Aleema Mirza Hamid (11)

An Example Of A True Teacher

I have a teacher who is an example for all
For all of you guys
Whether fat, thin, short or tall
She is a little strict, but very generous
She gives the best prizes to all
Whether good or envious

It is a true exemplary behaviour
For other teachers are not good
They aren't fair in judging
And can be in an extremely bad mood
If you want to become a teacher
Follow her example
So that you can teach like her
And be another fantastic example

She is a wonderful person with bright ideas
And encourages us all
When we lose hope and are in tears
It is the end of my Year 6
So I have to say goodbye to her

Well, she was an example
So I will respect and love her

So please listen to me, teachers!
Teach your students with love
And don't be belittlers!
I hope this'll inspire you, bye!

Hafsah Saleem (11)

My Sister

Mum always says she doesn't have favourites,
But we all know that she's the one.
Perfect wardrobe, perfect job.
And loved by everyone.
I wish I could be as strong,
As brave, as confident and kind,
When you meet her, you always remember.
Because one like her is hard to find.
The things she does for me are amazing.
Nobody will ever come close.
Perfect make-up, hair and fashion.
Although she does often boast.
Sometimes we fall out,
We fight like cat and dog.
But when we are we together
We're two peas in a pod.
When I'm with her I feel important.
Everyone knows she's got the best looks,
That's another thing she beats me at.
But she could do with reading some books.

Sometimes she gives me money.
She's given me my first job.
She told my parents I was good at it,
But said I need to shut my gob!
I could never imagine a life without her.
She's my idol, who I aspire to be.
Because if it wasn't for my sister,
I wouldn't be me.

Megan Amelia Eastwood (14)

Idol Poem

There are many people whom I idolise
From non-famous people
To celebrities all through time
But there is one person who inspires me a lot
As my idol, he takes top spot
My father has always been
An inspiration to me
I bet my mother would totally agree
By being there when I need help with my maths
And when something goes wrong,
He doesn't get a wrath
There are various times when he is humorous
But when he must be, he is very serious
Having an astute father is very great
He drops me at school
Even when he is late (for work)
When he sees that I am down
He turns into a smile
What once was a frown
When I talk to him he listens
And he also helps me with my division

There are many people whom I idolise
From non-famous people
To celebrities all through time
But my father is the one who inspires me a lot
As my idol, he takes top spot.

David Aderibigbe

A Bawse Is My Idol, The Official Guide

This is a person
That represents everything I believe in.
From world peace to no hunger,
To stopping gender inequality.
They define the word 'Bawse'
And stand against brutality.
They are hard to find in today's day of age
Since the creation of technology,
But I bet you they're there, sitting next to you,
If you take a look more closely.
Your mum, your nan,
Or even your brother's girlfriend could be one.
Ask them a couple of inspiring questions
and I'm sure they'll admit to being one.

There are many steps to being a Bawse,
Just check out
iiSuperwomanii's YouTube channel.
But here are the three main steps
That you must follow

Spread love to everyone
And try not to be hated.
Be kind and try to be yourself,
No matter who hates it.
So there you have it.
The official guide to being a Bawse.

Tinotenda Tekenende (12)

My Star Idol Mackenzie Ziegler - Dance Moms

M ackenzie is my star because she's unbreakable and nails all her dances (she works hard)
A nimating her face wins her all the competitions.
C ool personality
K ind and hard-working
E ntertaining performance, is why she's my idol.
N ever gives up.
Z esty, fun, thrilling and new dances.
I love her dance 'U no U love it'.
E ncourages her teammates.

Z ingy is her personality (that's what gives her that spark!) and that's why I would like to be like her.
I ntriguing in group dances and stands out; like in my favourite group dance (Kinky Boots: Lift me up)
E nchanting when she's on stage
G ifted with talent
L ittle but fierce!

E dgy style of dance
R estless (she's always dancing, like me).

Anya Main (10)

Role Model

My nan is the biggest role model
Anyone could ask for,
When we laughed the tears would pour,
My nan is so beautiful inside and out
She showed what caring is all about
She worked hard
And puts 100 percent into everything
She would always tell you what she would think
She made me feel so blessed
Because I knew I had the nan who was best
Whenever I was down
She would cheer me up the best she could
She did everything a perfect nan would
She always put others before herself
Was always willing to help
My nan inspires me
Because all her hard work she would commit to,
I bet Heaven has a very long queue
I will never forget my role model.
Thank you for everything, Nan
I've always been your number one fan

I want to be like her
The fact she's gone is just not fair.

Natalie Ann Hughes (18)

My Number One

One in a million, adored by all
Heart as big as the world or as high as I stand tall
Eyes as blue as the ocean
A smile that lights up a room
Withered hands that have worked long and hard
Skin as milky as the moon
Making people laugh or cry
Encouraging others to give everything a try
Dances like a crazy horse on a hot summer's day
Listens intently to every word I say
Voice as gentle and soft as cotton wool
Arms that wrap around me to keep me safe and warm
Sometimes acts a bit silly, pulling faces in the mirror
Takes selfies with her phone, expecting us to cheer
Talks for hours on the phone about this and that
Leaves the house in winter wearing a silly fluffy hat
Although she wears dark clothes, mainly blue or black
She still looks very pretty, there is no denying that

So, who is this special person, my world, my number one?
She is of course my amazing, super, funny mum.

Karla Elaine Shuttlewood (11)

Strings Or Justice?

His eyes are silver,
Like windows to the soul.
Staring at the enemies of humanity
While he raises his sword to fight our foes.
While he raises his shield to defend us,
He'll never fade away.

Their words are like knives
As they play with our lives,
But he hears our screams
And reaches his hand and raises us to battle.
He won't let them steal our freedom;
He won't let us be forgotten,
Written off as less than worthless
And trampled like flowers.

There's a wild fire in his heart
That can't be extinguished,
There are beings that live off our fears
They control you like they own you,
But he refuses,
His desires can't be extinguished.

Who is he?
The true spirit and embodiment of justice
Or just the ordinary man?

Benjamin Adam Wright

One True Idol

What can I say about my one true idol?
There's far too large an amount!
She made me,
She raised me,
She even taught me to count!

I don't remember much of our early days,
But I know they were loving.
Days of whining, and nights of screaming,
Yet she would never complain.

I'm still amazed at how she coped,
Cleaning, caring, and cooking,
Whilst we just sat and groaned.
She'd hoover the floor gracefully,
Yet we'd get mad at interruption to the TV.
She'd spend hours preparing a meal,
Yet we'd spit and yell, 'Ych a fi!'
She did so much for us every day and night,
Yet we took it for granted just as much.

Now I'm older,
I understand what she did.

I'm grateful and happy,
That she raised me like this.
There's no arguing,
And there's no denying,
That my mother is my one true idol.

Ewan Austin (17)

Words Spoken For Themselves

My idol is J K Rowling
With her gift of giving words life
Filled with colour and sounds
That could dance without any music played
Along the pages; as familiar as a friend
Across the black-inked pages
Breathing emotion into every letter
That of which then pair up into sentences
And paragraphs to chapters
Flowing when told to
And weaving delicately into plots
Like patchwork
Complying with her every notion
And coming together at last,
As seamlessly and smoothly
And harmoniously whole,
Like it was already meant to be.
The words speaking for themselves from her books
Loudly or quietly,
You can hear the words from the first to last page

But the brilliantly best moments are when
Its voice can still be heard,
And seen in your mind's eye
Even once you finish.

Fereshta Amiri (17)

Idol

Face as smooth as a baby's bottom,
Skin as clear as the Bodrum sea,
Hair braided and she is wearing all white,
Tears falling down our cheeks,
She looks like she is in a deep sleep,
But she is gone,
Dead,
That word plays in my head when I can't sleep,
The non-stop battle with my mind,
I miss her,
But she is gone,
I fake a smile and laugh with them,
They will never know about my pain,
The pain that hurts so bad I can't breathe,
But I know she is gone,
How do I cope?
How do I move on?
Does this grief end?

The voices reminding me she is gone and is never coming back

My cousin,
My princess,
My idol,
Left me and all these things she has done in nine years is amazing.

I miss her,
But she is gone,
She is just gone...

Halima Bahnan (13)

The Middlers

I idolize many people
But this one may surprise you
This isn't any one person
But a group of people

I call them the Middlers
The problem solvers
The ones who people ask
'Whyyy?'

The middle children,
Who never get attention
And aren't even able
To compete for it

The middle friends,
Stuck in-between two others
And their problems
And their situations

The middle students
Never praised for work

Never told off for behaviour
But always there, learning

I don't idolise these people
In the way I want to be
In their situations
But I do admire them

Their strength and stamina
Resilience and loyalty
If I could have that kind of confidence
When helping so many people

That's why I idolise the Middlers!

Isabelle Kimberley

J K Rowling

I'm inspired by J K Rowling,
I've even chose what team I might be in,
I've got the courage like a Gryffindor,
But the wisdom like a Ravenclaw.

I have the courage to complete tasks like a lion,
But I resolve problems with intelligence like a badger,
I think I'm a cross with them two,
I am lion-hearted and acceptant.

I'm inspired by J K Rowling,
I've even chose my wand trait,
It has the feather of a phoenix,
The wood is the pleasant pear tree.

For the warm-hearted,
People who are as soft as cotton,
For the resilient,
People who are as courageous as a valiant soldier.

J K Rowling inspired me,
I am glued to her books,
It holds me like I can never let go of it,
I idolise J K Rowling!

Asvitha Sarma (11)

My Idol

G reat
R andom
A mazing
N uts
D aring
M arvellous
A wesome

You may think I'm 90 for thinking this
But my nan
Is the man

She's gone through some tough times
But she hasn't gone sour like lemons and limes
She's still standing
And still baking

She's not strong physically
But mentally she's the strongest person ever
She's had cancer twice
And other things that can't be fixed with ice

So Grandma, I'm just gonna say
You make me who I am today
I love you so much
And not just because of your amazing lunch!

Emma Cartwright (11)

My Grandad I Miss You

I was told you had cancer,
Which made me really sad,
But didn't know you were that bad.

I thought Grandad, you would live for years
And only now can see you in my tears.

Using your fag papers as eyelashes
Making me laugh
And Mum cutting your toenails
Because they were so sharp.

I know you were poorly
And holding on for us all
And I wish you could just give us a call.

This might be selfish,
But I wish you were here
Or if only you could stay for one more year.

I miss you Grandad,
Every single day
And there is only one more thing for me to say

I love you Grandad.

Harrison Taylor Commons (15)

My Feelings Poem

I'm happy.
I'm so happy.
Like a flower blooming.
I'm sad.
I'm so sad.
Like a rain cloud raining.
I'm angry.
I'm so angry.
Like a thunder cloud flashing.
I'm excited!
I'm so excited!
Like it's a child's birthday
And the child is going to get a puppy.
I'm jealous.
I'm so jealous.
Like someone won a race
But the other team worked so hard.
I love you.
I really love you.
Like I have a rose
And it smells like a smelling candle

'I love it!' It smells like a daisy.
I hate you.
I really hate you.
As if an angry emoji punched you
Really hard in the heart.
As hard as it can.
And then all your feelings went.

Imogen Searles (7)

Super Shaz

Shaz, you are such a huge part of my life!
You were there
When I was in my mummy's tummy,
You were there when I was born,
You were there
To watch me: crawl, talk and walk,
You were there to celebrate
My first birthday and five more,
You were there
For my first day at nursery and school,
You were there
When I was ill, well and having fun,
You were there with me
For my first holiday and two more,
You were there to watch me grow.
That's why I just want to say
Thank you Shaz,
For being there for me as my aunty,
Mummy, sister, friend and buddy!

Aaria Bains (6)

Who Inspires Me?

The person who inspires me,
Is someone that I'd love to be.

Her first book was written in a cafe,
For her house was much too cold,
The word was spread around the world
Her story was told.

Her stories are imaginative and creative,
(She's written quite a few),
She's inspired many people,
Probably including you.

The reason she inspires me,
Though as young as I may be,
From a simple idea in her head
That grew and expanded like a spider's thread,
J K Rowling,
You write the best stories I've ever read!

Sarah Manning (11)

Mum

I know.
How typical.
'My mum:
The greatest person in the world'
But it's true.
Managing to work,
Raise four children,
Cook, and
Chauffeur each of us
To our individual hobbies,
Encouraged by,
You'll never guess who...
Mum!
Piano to dance
To ice hockey
And tutoring,
School and who knows where else.
Still managing to get through each day
Without a drop in her step.
Underappreciated.

Yet with unspoken emotions,
Tear-stained cheeks
Brushed by her soft and gentle fingers,
I see her pain.
Admiring her resilience for us to succeed.
Her love.
Burning a million holes
In the darkened sky
For the sun to shine through.

Georgia Clarice Paxton-Doggett (17)

Rosanna Pansino

Rosanna Pansino is an awe-inspiring baker,
She is funny, great and is an amazing maker.
Cupcakes, cake pops, candies too,
So many to try out for me and you.
I adore her baking tips
When I tried making a milkshake
And took a sip.
I love her attitude towards baking cakes,
But wait till you see what she can make.
She inspires me to start baking
And I love how she does her decorating.
I want to be just like her
And make some batter and give it a stir.
She is my idol that you can say,
I wish I could meet her
Somehow, I just need a way.

Ayesh Mohsin

My Idol

Martin Luther King Jr: a brilliant man,
For black civil rights, he made a stand.
Martin Luther, no one he would despise,
And everyone was equal, at least in his eyes.
In Atlanta, Martin was born and raised,
And it was only Jesus that he praised.
Some people, though, didn't like his words,
They killed him and sent him to another world.
His dreams live on till the end of existence,
To inspire someone, like me, for instance.
Some heroes stand unnoticed,
Some heroes like to stand tall,
But Martin Luther in my eyes,
Was the best of them all!

Dami Daniel Olawoye (13)

Friendships Are Like...

Friendships are like flowers,
As some die off,
But some stay alive,

Friendships are like insects,
Some are mega annoying,
But some are precious,

Friendships are like tissues,
Some will break apart,
But some will remain strong,

Friendships are like songs,
As some may fail,
But some will succeed,

Friendships are like pens,
As some may run out,
But some will always continue,

Friendships are like books
Some have a fast ending,
But some are never ending

Friendships are like you and me,
Love, hope, courage and devotion,
That's what makes me whole.

Kiera Douglas

Shakespeare's Work

The work of Shakespeare is special
And he did not just write plays,
That man also wrote poems
And it took him more than days.
If I met Shakespeare
I imagine him being quite nice,
If I had the chance to meet him
I wouldn't think twice.
Poems and plays,
What a busy man!
If he thought he could do it,
I guess I can.
From romance and tragedy
To history and comedy,
He put it all together
And made a good job.
He made words like thee and thou
But I invented the word 'thingiemabob!'

Sophie Lucketti (10)

My Idol

My idol is amazing,
She has the abilities to make me smile,
She can even make me go to sleep.
I wish to be an amazing cook,
A meal which the whole world enjoys.
I wish to be a phenomenal washer,
Who can make clothes shine like diamonds.
I wish to be a fabulous stylist,
Who knows every single style.
I wish to be a creative writer,
Who can make shocking stories on the spot.
I wish to be a quick-witted driver,
Who can go anywhere in a flash.
I wish to be my mum,
Who stands by me through thick and thin.

Kethusha Saseestharan (13)

Sisters

Strong, beautiful, proud
A sister I love
Paisley, kind and sweet
Ella, different and wonderful
In a world they are perfect
They fit right in
I love them dearly
One perfect for my heart
They fix it together
When it is broken down
They bring a smile to my face
Different from an ordinary smile
Playing all day
They make new friends
I am always one of them
When they are broken down
I get them up and bring a smile to their faces
They love me dearly
I make tonnes of friends
But they will always be one

We are like a rock
We never break
Sisters
Make
The
Best
Of
Friends!
They always do!

Laurel Smith (13)

Whatever

'Whatever!'
My sister would say.
'Whatever!' we'd hear
All night, all day.

'Whatever!'
She would kill us with the line.
'Whatever!'
All the time.

'Whatever!'
She would bore us.
'Whatever!'
Did she expect more from us?

'Whatever!'
Did she have mental health problems?
'Whatever!'
Did she want us to solve them?

'Whatever!'
How rude!
'Whatever!'
Then she met a dude.

They went off,
Got wed.
Then I got her room
And her bed.

'Whatever!'
I miss her so much.

Tasnim Adan (11)

Where Did Santa Go?

I sit by my window waiting, waiting
Midnight on the 24th of December
No satsumas in the stockings
No candy canes on the bed frame
What does this mean?
Is it all just a dream?

I run down the stairs
And into the living room
The cookies and milk are still on the desk

No presents under the trees
No fun
No laughter
No Christmas

There are tears
There is sadness
Why is it not a sensation?
Is this my imagination?

Where did Santa go?

Somi Angel Ramona Ejiro Enaife (11)

My Mother

She's there when I need her,
She's there when I don't,
She's there always comforting me,
Helping me to persevere,
And be myself.

My mother,
Is ever so pretty,
Her skin is as soft as a baby's bottom,
And her hair is as soft as fur,
Her smile is brighter than the sun,
One glimpse and you're blind!

Her eyes twinkle in the moonlight,
When you gaze into her eyes you see her true
Loyalty and beauty.

That's my mother,
I'm not ashamed to say it,
I never will be,
That's why I love her,
That's why she loves me.

Esther Kaombe Ngwewa (9)

A Sonnet To My Mum

You are the person I most admire,
I hope to be as brilliant as you.
As I grow older, I do aspire,
To be beautiful and wonderful too.

My shopping buddy, my very best friend,
My loving mum, my greatest role model.
I love my priceless time with you, we spend
Hours talking, baking, sewing, crafting.

You are here for me, every day and night,
You always have been and always will be.
Lighting up the dark like a beam of light,
Your advice and love calm every worry.

Thank you for every little thing you do,
I love you, every little part of you.

Jessica Downe (14)

Untitled

My brother, my aspiration,
The one who never knows my admiration.
He works some days,
And plays all night.

He likes to give me a fright,
But doesn't succeed, try as he might.
I'll miss him,
When he's not home.

We always go on holiday,
Though he may not want it that way.
We are friends,
Though we don't act it.

My brother is my best friend,
And I never want it to end.
I would love to be like him,
He is living a type of dream.

Hollie Mae Tapper (15)

Sister

Her head kind of looked like an egg.
All round and shiny,
You could see the cerebral yolk
Inside.

She came out kicking and screaming...
You could hear her on the other side
Of the canvassed corridor.
Awake. Definitely awake.

You seemed to look at peace,
As if Mum's screeches were worth it.
You instantly sublimed
From sleep to wake.

The midwife flicked away
The remnants of the ordeal.
You had specks of hair
Littering your head.
A sprinkle of salt ingrained.

That was when I knew,
Life would never be the same again...

Udit Mahalingam

Brothers

My brothers are my heroes
The definition of bravery are my brothers
They are out there inspiring loads of people
Wearing a simple smile,
Not a frown ever to be seen.

Their smiles can light up a mile
Their love for me is as pure as a dove.

When it comes to defending family
They have the heart of a lion.

They have though, a side
That is motivated by love and affection,
Respect and pride in all they do.

They will always be my heroes.

Mariam Khan (12)

The Power Of Mother-Mama Mooshk

Hair the colour of rust
and eyes the colour of rain
Green, blue, grey - a world ahead
a world behind of silver mist, sadness and tears
of smoke in the eyes.
Or the freshness of iridescent dew
upon glowing skin like white-hot metal
The birth, the forgery of a star of passion
Visible in the condensation glittering in the eyes
Wet electricity crackle! And spark!
Behind a world of burning fire and lime
burnishing the skull, inhuman-like the magnificent hues
of explosions of hair. Cooling to rust.
Hot to the touch.

Katie Stewart (18)

My Inspiration/Idol

They asked me one day who my inspiration is
I paused as my throat began to clam up
because you came to my mind
they asked again one more time
I said my inspiration you all won't know
yet she taught me everything I know
she made me laugh when I swore I couldn't
she made me feel like I could fly
yet she passed and barely anyone knew her
but to me she will always be a part of my identity
you see when they asked me who is my inspiration,
only you came to my mind.

Sophie Louise Evans (14)

Idols

I dols are to inspire.
D on't worry, people are there to inspire you.
O nly think about your success.
L ots of people can become idols, including you.
S tay focused on the right path.

F riends or family can also be idols,
A nd teachers too.
M y idol is my family.
I really like my family.
L et the idol inspire you.
Y ou have to find the right idol for you.

Rahul Vijay Singh (9)

Grandpa

Oh, Grandpa, how grateful I can be,
You just make me, *me*.
Holding me tight as I open my wings,
A happiness that just clings.
You'll get through it,
You won't want to sit.
You'll go jogging on,
To running a marathon.
You gave me courage when I was low,
And now it's going to show.
As lucky as I'll ever be,
I jump for joy and scream with glee!
I love you lots,
Stuffed into pots,
I'll love you no matter how,
'Cos you'll be with me forever now.

Maria Manta (12)

Mum

You're there when I need you
That's never a doubt
You're there when I'm trying
To work things out
You're there when I'm troubled
You're there when I'm sad
You're there when things,
Are looking so bad
You tell me you love me
You give me advice
For no reason you hug me
Which is always so nice
Mum, I do love you
Mum, I do care
Especially knowing
You'll always be there.

Alaha Baig (11)

The Old Doll

Her black eyes are made of beads,
But they're the only ones she needs,
And she has no hair at all,
For she's just an old rag doll
From an old school.

Her best dress is very plain,
She's been out in the rain,
And her age I mustn't tell,
Even though I know it very well.

But I love this one the best,
Better than all the rest,
And I hug her very tight,
And I love her day and night.

Zoe Lewis (9)

My Canine Coach

The tough times I've been through, you were there
You scared off the fears that held me back, with a stare
I've realised through the years that happiness comes from you
And all those walks with you in the summer dew,
By doing your little woof, I started laughing
And you became my companion, which was enchanting
You are more than a small creature
You are my feelings' teacher
I have yet to learn other things
But I have you, so I thank God for such blessings.

Rishika Singh (14)

Motivational Mother

Who better to ask than my mother?
She has all the answers, saves me the bother.
She motivates me to be the best,
I have seen her work and she'll never rest,
She brought me up, took care of me,
There's nothing that I could do
To repay this love,
I aspire to be like her,
And strive to be the best,
What would I do without my fantastic mother?
Words that I cannot express,
All I can say is...
Thank you Mother!

Bareerah Chughtai (13)

Jaqueline Wilson

J ust the right story
A mazing techniques
Q uestions answered
U nique style
E verything is realistic
L ives are touched
I n a new land
N ever afraid
E verlasting wisdom

W e are enlightened
I am speechless
L ots of emotion
S ense of reality
O ften a book you can't put down
N othing is the same.

Amalia Maria Mitrovici (12)

How Am I Supposed To Know?

Who do I idolise,
my mum or dad or a pop star perhaps?
How am I supposed to know?
Too many people, too many ghosts.
All I need is one
the one that can teach me what has to be done,
to change the world and surprise,
Now that I won't despise
I know there is someone out there
a teacher, a fighter, a constructor
just hope I'll find someone,
someone I can call my idol.
How am I supposed to know?

Monica Mustapha

My Sock Idol

I love my beautiful, handsome sock,
I wear it every single place I go,
It is as pretty as the prettiest frock,
I always seem to put it on show.

I cherish my sock with all my love,
And I'm it's number one fan,
Sometimes I even use it as a glove,
It even has a perfect tan.

It has been my friend since I were born,
I think it is the best sock ever,
Yes, It's definitely the best sock I've worn,
I will always love it forever...

Josh Takhi (13)

Idols

Idols, there's not just one...
In this world, there are many,
Many, who inspire you,
You are inspired,
Inspired by those,
Those like your parents, who,
Who are close to your heart, but,
But they can be your teachers,
Teachers who guide you,
You to take the right steps,
Steps that you take,
Take to shape your future,
Future is yours,
Yours to be inspired,
Inspired by those,
Those who you say are your idols,
Idols, there's not just one...

Priya Vijay Singh (14)

Women In Blue

In the finals of the ICC Women's Championship, these legendary women have tried their best
To make the people of India happy.
Never have these inspiring women given up in a single match
Doing their job excellently, the cricketers have impressed all of us
Indians at heart, they have played for their nation
Always persevering, these amazing women have never lost hope
Hats off to the Indian Women Cricket Team.

Vedika Hemanth Gowda (11)

My Dad Is Amazing And Funny

My dad is amazing and funny,
But he is nothing like a bunny.
He does lots of farts,
He knows nothing about darts.
His name is Ken,
And he has also made a den.
We run around the block,
And we're on the clock.
We play around with balls,
He makes lots of calls.
We go out on my bike to the park,
And stay there till it is dark.
He loves karate,
He likes going to a party.
My dad is number 1,
And is always lots of fun.

Joshua Wagner (9)

My Idol!

My mum is amazing and treats us all day long,
You might think my mum is just an ordinary mum but actually she is the opposite of ordinary,

Interesting but funny jokes Mum likes to share with the family,
Determined to make us happy,
Over and over, making sure every one of us is alright,
Love, care and protect is what she does best.

Alice Burns (11)

I Can't Wait 'Til Christmas

C hrist was born on this day
H e is the best thing that happened to the world
R ed, white and blue wrapping paper
I just can't wait 'til Christmas
S tockings hung from the fireplace
T alking about Christmas face-to-face
M y family singing around the tree
A s I open presents happily
S o I can't just wait 'til Christmas.

Sineidin Serlom Tamakloe

My Nanny

Love means Nanny,
My nanny is my hero,
I've seen her from zero,
Nanny's our family queen,
Respect Nanny all the time,
She's beautiful than a sunrise,
Nanny gives gifts like Santa,
When Nanny is with me,
It's like I'm a joey,
When Nanny is with family,
We start our home orchestra,
I love those days.

Rithika Raghunandanan (8)

My Idol

My idol is my dad,
Mum says he can be quite bad.
I think he is funny and silly,
He keeps me warm when it is chilly.
He picks me up when I fall down,
And tells me not to frown.
He is a better cook than my mum,
He makes doing chores lots of fun.
He is my taxi, my cook, my nurse,
He even puts money in my purse.
I love my dad so so much.
No offence Mum, but Dad is my number 1.

Hope Stokes (11)

My Dear Granny

She has a sweet face,
but a slow pace.
She is old,
nearly bald.
Every time she comes,
I look at her ancient thumbs,
her little pinkies
that hurts when she winkies.
She eats a fruit a day,
so her teeth don't decay.
All day she prays,
but she still has time to play.

Have you guessed?
They are your and my best.
It's Grandma but...
The one with proper grammar.

Derin Ester Iyapo (10)

The Supervet

Noel Fitzpatrick is an intelligent man
He always has a thought-out plan
He helps in lots of different ways
That will sometimes keep animals in for days
If something goes wrong
He will always improvise
Noel Fitzpatrick is very good at saving lives
So this is why I look up to him
I want to save so many lives
Just like he does.

Freya Anderson (8)

David Walliams

The world's best book seller.
Hilarious, amusing, ridiculous,
Like a constantly sneezing cat.
As extraordinarily delightful
As eating chocolate for the rest of your life.
He is a daft dog dozing.
He makes me feel excited,
Like a buzzing bee in a field full of flowers.
David Williams,
The light of everyone's day.

Samuel Osborn (9)

My Baby Sister

My baby sister screams in delight,
My baby sister doesn't sleep at night.

My baby sister chews all day,
My baby sister loves to play.

My baby sister is usually cheerful,
My baby sister is sometimes tearful.

My baby sister splashes in the bath,
My baby sister makes me laugh.

My baby sister loves to crawl,
My baby sister is the cutest of all.

Eliza Shearn (7)

Min Yoongi

Maybe it's the way you smile
Or the way you laugh
You'll always see me as a fan
But I'll always see you as an idol

Yes, you speak another language
But that doesn't stop me
From learning what I can
To understand your lyrics

You've had the world upon your shoulders
Yet you still reached the top
Making your own path
As you are Min Yoongi.

Freya Butler (13)

Peter Pan

Second star beyond the skies,
Above the destiny lies,
Cloud of green shall be seen,
Emerald eyes hit the seas,
Fights pirates with the bee's knees,
Lost boys obey their leader, whose voice chills,
Moment burning without a kill,
Faith, trust and pixie dust,
For they live in Neverland,
He is Peter Pan.

Sehrish Malik

Grandad

Oh, I love my grandad,
He used to call me Son
And to be fair he did treat me like one,
He like the chocolate called Fry's,
Every time I had to go I always kissed him goodbye.

When we walked in he cheered up,
He also sat up,
He made me smile,
Even from a mile.

He made me laugh and cry,
RIP Grandad,
I wish you hadn't died.

Ryan King

Who My Idol Is

My uncle is who my idol is,
We play games and have a lot of fun,
But of course, when it comes to my siblings, he is for everyone,
He inspires me to try different things like this,
Our favourite thing to play is an obscure little card game,
And he picks me up even in the rain,
When he's around I never dawdle,
And that is why he is my idol.

Benjamin Robert Francis Fletcher (13)

Love My Idol

Haiku poetry

Lamp guiding the way
Candle lighting up my world
I love my idol

Encouraging me
Silently supporting me
I love my idol

My wings; let me fly
My parachute; catching me
I love my idol

My home, my safe place
The one who believed in me
I love my idol.

Armaan Mohammed (14)

Who Is My Idol?

Idol, idol, who is my idol?
To a musician or author,
Who do I idolise?
To a baker
To an actress
To a singer
Who is my idol?
Could it be a boy band
Or girl band?
Who is my idol?
Bruno Mars, Olly Murs
Or Katy Perry, Taylor Swift.
Who is my idol?
I really don't know.

Sophie Parsons (9)

Same Name, Different Person, But My Inspiration

Maddie Ziegler is my idol
Her dreams get bigger and bigger
But what I never can quite figure
Is how she is so gracious and kind
And has a thoughtful mind
So when I try a new thing
I won't give up on everything
Because I think of her and what she's done
And in the end my job is done.

Maddie Bradfield (9)

The Better One

I have no spite for you,
Like others may claim,
No corrupting jealousy,
For the words you tame.
I am only in awe,
For the lives you change,
For the friends you create,
No matter how strange.
I will always walk in your shadow,
But do not think badly,
For the places it will take me,
I will live in it gladly.

Nina Holguin

Everything!

The sunshine to light my day,
The person to tell me everything is OK,
You always know what to say.

You're always there to support me,
And we all do agree,
Now you're a mother of three,
You're proof that a mum is what you're supposed to be

You're my mum,
And I love you.

Karen Kou (10)

My Daddy

I love my daddy,
Very strong and tall.
I love my daddy
He never has a pain at all!

I love my daddy
He will always be there
I love my daddy because,
He will always be there to answer my call!

Yes, I love my daddy
He loves me too,
And I love him,
And you should love yours too!

Leah Young (11)

I Will Always Remember You

Gran, you made me happy,
That's why I'm blue
I'll always be there
Just like you were too
You're no longer here
But my memories of you
Are always in my heart
Along with you
I will always love you.

Lucyanne Reid (16)

To A Teacher

I know I'm not the brightest,
Sometimes I don't have a clue, not the slightest,
But you help me get through.
For this alone I thank you.
Sometimes when I doubt myself
I remember your encouraging words,
Smile and
Am filled with determination.

Molly Emery (16)

Barack Obama

I admire Obama
For many reasons wide
One of them is...
That he made America fly
He turned the USA into a smile
Well, only for a little while
He really is my idol
Has he been in a river so tidal?

Joanna Ezeonu (9)

My Inspirations

She always thinks about me first,
Though I am sometimes at my worst
Always puts food on my plate
And never arrives at school late.

She might be firm, she might be tough,
See right through me and not be rough,
Though she might scream and even shout,
She'll never ever show me out
Her lovely massive, creamy house,
Where it's never quiet like a mouse.

Now him the strong, the Superman,
No heart of steel; my number one fan,
He keeps me safe and checks I'm fine,
Especially when I am online.

I might be moody, I might be down,
He'll sing a song from Motown,
We have much fun messing about
Going round and round the roundabout.
He might get stressed and never rest,
Working hard to give me the best.

They are everything to me,
My life, my world, a special key,
They love me, care for me,
Don't want me to leave
Even when I turn eighteen.

They are the best, amazing too,
They are fantastic and that's true.
I cannot wait each time to see
Their faces when they come to me.
I am proud and I am glad
They truly are my mum and dad.

Danai Symona Mushambi (10)
Cranbourne Primary School, Winkfield

The Person Who Inspires Me

The person who inspires me is not a sports star,
Or a celebrity, by far,
They make you happy
And they never make you cry,
And when you can't sleep,
They sing you a lullaby.

They are good and kind and gentle and sweet,
When you were young,
They told you what to wear and eat,
They will always be proud and hold you close,
And whatever you do wrong,
They will love you the most.

Always love them, as they will love you,
When you came into the world brand new,
The world can be sweet and it can be sour,
They will love you more by the hour.

Always love everyone and always love yourself,
They will look after you
When you have got bad health

And when you hurt yourself
They will always come,
Because this person (of course)
Has to be your mum!

Thank you Mum for all you have done for me.
I love you.

Flo Taylor (10)
Cranbourne Primary School, Winkfield

My Mum And Dad

My mum and dad, they're the best people ever,
They are extremely kind and very clever,
They support you through the roughest times,
They tell you to never go out
And cause the crimes.

My mother, she's the happiest person on Earth,
She can shout, she can be firm
When I'm not as good as good,
With my homework she'll help me learn,
My mother, she's the best ever.

My father, he's the funniest man
In the universe,
He keeps me safe, he keeps me near,
He says he'll never let me go
And I should always go for my hopes,
He's done that himself,
My father, he's the best man ever.

My parents mean the world to me,
They hug me and kiss me,
And help me grow

They lead me through life the right way,
My parents mean the world to me.

Lauren Ellis (9)
Cranbourne Primary School, Winkfield

Gandhi

Gandhi was a truly amazing man,
He showed that no one owns their own land,
We are all a working group together,
We should never be on opposite sides.

He led everyone through hard times,
I think he is amazing to do so,
And even if your actions are bad
He would never rank them low,
As long as you are sorry.

When India was in trouble,
He stepped in and tried to make it better,
And he made families less upset,
And he will always be remembered
As a brave treasure.

This just proves that anyone
Can do what they like,
And you should always live up to your dreams,
But you should always help people who need it,
And you should especially help
The world you live in.

Amrita Charan Evans (9)
Cranbourne Primary School, Winkfield

Liz Pichon

I think Liz Pichon is cool,
Even though she was not the top in school,
She is very good at tricks,
I do wonder how she thinks,
She makes my imagination run wild,
She must have been a mad child.

Even though when writing books she takes forever,
I still think she is very clever,
I love reading her books all the way,
I hope another Tom Gates book comes out today,
Thinking I want to be like her,
All day lying on the sofa.

I try to think of mad ideas,
But I keep thinking of the meatballs at Ikea,
I'm still full of hope,
But can I think of ideas, nope!
I think that Liz Pichon is cool,
She should have been the top in school.

Evelyn Fraser (10)
Cranbourne Primary School, Winkfield

Parents

My parents are amazing,
My parents are great,
They're amazing, they're great
And what is more, they're very lovely.

Take us to the cinema,
Take us to the restaurant,
They prepare fun days out,
Lots of laughing; lots of love.

When I'm feeling at my worst,
They always seem to burst out and help,
Even when I was a baby,
Also through childhood.

When I was naughty, when I was a pest,
They always seemed to love me,
They thought I was the best.

I love my mum and dad,
They get me treats when I'm good.

I love them lots and lots,
And it's good that whatever I do
They always love me too.

Harry Graham Dommett (11)
Cranbourne Primary School, Winkfield

Tony Ross

He is short but neat,
And in an art contest,
He can never be beaten.

He draws for Clare Balding,
Roald Dahl too,
He draws to his heart's desire,
He draws trees, even fire!

Tony Ross is an artist, you can't deny it,
And if you want his artwork, you have to buy it.
He draws for loads of authors,
Loads of exciting authors!

Tony Ross is a massive inspiration,
He makes up words like 'galleiation',
You have to love Tony Ross,
He is definitely the boss!

30 lines is all he writes,
No fairy tales and he will not fight!

But art is in his heart.
Like mine.
Together we can never be beaten.

Isabelle Perkins (10)
Cranbourne Primary School, Winkfield

Taylor Swift!

Taylor sings like an angel,
Her songs sound like a bird tweeting,
She is as sweet as sugar,
And is as pretty as flowers.

She always tries her best,
And never ever has a rest,
Taylor will never give up,
And loves her pup.

She is full with glee,
And fans buzz around her like bees,
Taylor is very clever,
And has to be the best singer ever.

She is extremely kind,
Her songs are always in my mind,
She has written lots of songs,
That don't sound like bongs.

I have never met her,
However, she is all the things that I want to be

She has a successful career,
And if I'm like her I will be OK.

Ellie Wishart-Core (9)
Cranbourne Primary School, Winkfield

Mum And Dad

If bad, if good, they are very great,
They give you a house
And put food on your plate,
They love us with all their heart,
Even from the very start,
When I am as awful as can be,
They will still love me,
They encourage me to be the best I can,
They will still encourage me
When I'm a full-grown man,
They will love me to the end of my life,
They help me through trouble and strife,
They teach me to be kind and polite,
Not to be mean and tight,
Mum and Dad are the best,
They're better than all the rest,
If I feel down,
Mum and Dad will get rid of my frown,
Thank you Mum and Dad,
Now I never feel bad.

Logan Horsley (10)
Cranbourne Primary School, Winkfield

Lionel Messi

Lionel Messi is my inspiration,
He is a football sensation,
He's played football for many years,
He's scored many goals
And has heard many cheers.

He plays football for Barcelona
And his country, Argentina,
He's scored more than 500 goals,
He can control the ball in small areas
And can pass super accurately.

Messi has won the World Cup once,
He hasn't played football for months,
He's been playing it for years,
He is fast and small
And is full of energy every match,
There are many reasons why
He is an inspiration to me,
I want to be the best footballer I can be.

Mikey Verga (10)
Cranbourne Primary School, Winkfield

My Mum!

This person is for life,
This person has no strife,
This person is very caring,
She is also sharing.

She is also very fun,
I love my mum a tonne,
My mum is very kind,
If I ask her she won't mind.

My mum is very clever,
She is the best mum ever,
My mum is very happy,
When she asks something she wants it snappy.

She is sometimes sad,
She is quite mad,
She is not that angry though,
She doesn't like to show.

She sometimes yells,
She says, 'Stop ringing those bells.'

She wants us to be quiet,
She loves the colour violet.

Hunnie Louise Crump (10)
Cranbourne Primary School, Winkfield

Emma Watson

Emma Watson is my hero,
Once her life was at zero,
Got bullied,
Her dream came true.

Acting for life,
Hermione Granger for life,
Emma's not bad,
And she never gets mad.

Now she is all grown up,
She gets a lot of luck,
Played Belle in Beauty and the Beast,
The star called Emma Watson.

She is using her fame,
Fighting for women's rights,
That is why she is my hero,
Civil rights,
Other people's and my own rights.

Emma Watson is my hero,
Once her life was at zero,
Got bullied,
Then her dream came true.

Poppy Alice Jackson (10)
Cranbourne Primary School, Winkfield

My Parents

My parents are amazing,
They're super encouraging,
They care about me,
Extremely amazingly,
They think about me first greatly from birth.

I'm really glad he is my dad,
He is definitely the opposite of bad,
He cares about my learning,
Even though I can sometimes be concerning,
He thinks I'm the best,
Even when he sits at his desk.

Sarah is the most supreme person I know,
She watched me learn and grow,
She is really smart,
And loves me from the heart,
She brought two cats into my life,
Because she is extremely nice.

Ollie Riley (10)
Cranbourne Primary School, Winkfield

Mum And Dad

Mum and Dad made me feel glad,
Even when I felt bad,
Mum said I'm not dumb,
Dad helped me
When I went through things that were bad,
They both said I was the best,
Even though I was a pest.

Mum and Dad helped me
When I went through things that were rough,
So I listened, and I stayed tough,
I loved them enough, I kissed them goodnight,
Then I held my teddy tight,
Whilst my mum turned off the light.

Mum and Dad made me glad,
Even when I felt bad,
Cheers Mum, cheers Dad,
For being the best parents ever to be had.

Max Roy Cantrell-Bennett (10)
Cranbourne Primary School, Winkfield

Manuel Neuer

I am inspired by Manuel Neuer,
He makes loads of great saves,
He looks like a beast in goal,
I don't know anyone
Who has scored a goal against him.

Every match he is full of energy,
Ready to win again,
He is ready for everything,
But not to be beaten.

He goes to training every day,
Just to get better,
Manuel Neuer gets better
And better every day,
To do hard and easy saves
Every day, even today.

Thomas Atack (10)
Cranbourne Primary School, Winkfield

Ronaldo

I think Ronaldo is a skill master,
He can't get any faster,
He makes my football life wild,
He must have been a mad child.

Even though he trains forever,
He is still very clever,
Even though when he loses and cries,
He will still play for his guys.

He keeps trying and he's got many skills,
He is rich but he still has to pay bills,
I think Ronaldo is cool
Even though he might not be the best.

George Jones (11)
Cranbourne Primary School, Winkfield

Emily Davison

My idol is Emily Davison
She helped women vote
Fighting for feminism
Struggling to gain attention

So at the king's race
A split second decision
Jumped in front of the king's horse
Killed on the course

Emily Davison
A strong-minded woman
Thank you for helping women to vote.

Katie Grant
Eastwood High School, Newton Mearns

Untitled

She has the skills,
She's made a deal
To play for Chelsea
To win the trophies.
Everyone knows
That when she scores
She goes crazy
And they are amazing.
She scores the goals in the finals,
She is the best
But when she's a beast
You can't stop her.
This is the England and Chelsea player
Gemma Davison.

Renai Bennett (12)
Hampton College, Hampton Vale

My Dad Is My Idol...

My dad is my idol
Because of the amazing person he is.
My dad is my idol
Because he grew up
In a small, poor village in South Africa.
My dad is my idol
Because he played rugby as a child barefoot
Because his parents couldn't afford shoes.
My dad is my idol
Because playing rugby got him
A scholarship to a university.
My dad is my idol,
Because he is the only one in our family
To go to university.
My dad is my idol
Because he had to study hard,
As he had less than most people
At the university.
My dad is my idol
Because he graduated from university
And became a quantity surveyor

Something most people haven't heard of.
My dad is my idol
Because he walked into
One of the biggest construction companies
In South Africa and got a job.
My dad is my idol
Because he fell in love and married my mom.
My dad is my idol
Because just after they got married
He got a job in the United Kingdom
And immigrated.
My dad is my idol because he is so amazing
That he opened his own company
Twelve years later.
The reason why my dad is my idol
Is because he is amazing, funny,
Smart and special...
He is one of a kind...
And he is my dad.

Toni Carla Van Wyk (12)
Hampton College, Hampton Vale

Best Friends

They are my best friends,
Two people who made my life amend,
When I'm happy or sad, moody or mad
They always seem to have my back,
The sleepovers and midnight snacks,
Girly things like that,
Painting nails and stupid tales,
But that is what friends are for,
My idols are these two people
Who make me who I am today.

Isabel Olivia Grainger (12)
Hampton College, Hampton Vale

Kwebbelkop

Kwebbelkop is my favourite person
Because I like to watch him on YouTube
He plays games and says funny names
He is very funny and makes a lot of money
I like to watch his videos every day
Because it is interesting to hear
What he has got to say
He has big hair
But he gets nightmares
I like to play games where I'm a soldier
I want to be like him when I'm older.

Elias Holm Johansen (9)
Mayfair International Academy, Estepona

My Hero, Kieren

My brother, Kieren, is my hero,
He was twenty when I was zero.
He's kind and brave, strong and funny,
He loves to visit me in Spain, because it's sunny.
We have fun adventures and he makes me tree swings,
He's always teaching me really cool things.
My brother is a policeman and very brave,
But he is never grumpy and will always wave.
I love my big brother.

Alfie Irvine (9)
Mayfair International Academy, Estepona

Kieron

K ieron
I s
E xcellent
R ealistic
O utstanding
N ice.

Suraj Robson Singh
Mayfair International Academy, Estepona

My Dad

My dad is loving
My dad is kind
He is so awesome
He has an open mind
I love the way he sings
I love his music and guitar
The way he makes me smile
The way he drives his car
Sometimes he's so hardworking
Sometimes he needs a rest
The point is he never gives up
And that's the bit I like the best
My dad's name is Christian
Christian Nicholas Halls
He is my loving father
And he likes to play with footballs!

Bethany Halls (9)
The Compass Primary Academy, Kettering

Maddison

Maddison has dark black hair.
Maddison has a purple jumper.
It has a compass.
Maddison is a wonderful girl with brown eyes.
She is my best friend
And we play together nearly every day.
She helps me with my work.
She comes to me and gives me big hugs
Like a sister.
She makes me feel like I'm her brother.
She makes me feel like we are in a flying castle
And I am the king
And Maddison is the queen.

Matthew Ellis (9)
The Compass Primary Academy, Kettering

About A Friend

Good friend
Likes hockey
Being good at all times
Wearing a tie smartly
Thinks about me as family
Favourite toy, trains as usual

Likes spending time with me
And others.

Always has time
When I want to play with him.

And his name
Is Austin Connolly.

His age is nine
So am I.

Favourite artist
Vincent van Gogh.

Gvidas Jakutavicius (10)
The Compass Primary Academy, Kettering

Lady Limelight

Good singer
Good dancer
Looks great
Clean teeth
Wears funky clothing
Never drinks coffee, drinks tea
No animals
Loves animals
Scared of tarantulas
Always has make-up on
Plays on, dances, dances and dances
Blue eyes
Very, very nice.

Lady Gaga!

Olivia Whitney (8)
The Compass Primary Academy, Kettering

My Idol

The only one I have
I always go to her for help
A very big part of my life
She's there when I need help
She cares for me and I care for her
The first person I go to
She has short, black hair
She is great to hug
Has the same skin tone as me
She has freckles.
My mum.

Hannah Marindire (10)
The Compass Primary Academy, Kettering

Mum And Ariana Grande

My mum is a great cook
My mum can do her own hair
My mum is great at handwriting
My mum is nice
My mum helps me decorate
My mum is great

Great singer
Great voice
She is in my three favourite movies
Good songs
Great band
She is great.

Paige Brennan (8)
The Compass Primary Academy, Kettering

Untitled

He is beautiful.
He looks after me and my mum loves him.
He's a boy and he lives with me.
He is a mechanic and I am inspired by him.
He earns money so we can go on holiday.
He plays with me.
I love him and my family loves him too.
It's my dad!

Theo Reed (8)
The Compass Primary Academy, Kettering

Untitled

Bad singer
Really funny
Really jokey
Wears good clothing
Very kind
Helps a lot
Loves tea
Very noisy
Loves turtles
Blue eyes
Brown hair
Good-looking
Very nice.

My brother.

Princess Rhiannon Bowes (9)
The Compass Primary Academy, Kettering

Untitled

He is incredible
He is very good at football
He looks after me
My mum loves him, so does my dad
He has blonde hair and blue eyes
I love him too
He plays for a football team
His name is Ryan.

Logan John Cross (9)
The Compass Primary Academy, Kettering

Mammy

M ammy takes care of me.
A best friend is always there for me when I need it.
M ammy and me.
M ammy and me.
Y ou and me will always be together forever.

Ruby Sabrina Birkett (8)
The Compass Primary Academy, Kettering

My Mum And Dad

My mum and dad
They look after me
They take care of me
They make me laugh all the time
They make me happy
They make me my favourite dinner
My mum and dad are my heroes.

Charlie Frost (8)
The Compass Primary Academy, Kettering

My Brother

My brother is the best.
My brother beats the rest.
He is little and small
But still is very cool.
He is very cute
When he is wearing boots.

Simrah Kaur
The Compass Primary Academy, Kettering

Footballer

Footballer
Plays for Man United
Has good skills
Name starts with I
He's a striker
His name is Ibrahimovic.

Tyler Bugg (8)
The Compass Primary Academy, Kettering

Untitled

Best scorer
Fast player
Midfielder
Manchester United
Yellow shoes
Paul Pogba
French player.

Ali Abdullah (10)
The Compass Primary Academy, Kettering

My Parents

Braver
Magical
Lovely
Funnier
Brown hair
Darker hair
Merrier
Wonderful
Kind.

Aaliyah Melton (9)
The Compass Primary Academy, Kettering

Young Writers Information

We hope you have enjoyed reading this book – and that you will continue to in the coming years.

If you're a young writer who enjoys reading and creative writing, or the parent of an enthusiastic poet or story writer, do visit our website **www.youngwriters.co.uk**. Here you will find free competitions, workshops and games, as well as recommended reads, a poetry glossary and our blog.

If you would like to order further copies of this book, or any of our other titles, then please give us a call or visit **www.youngwriters.co.uk**.

Young Writers
Remus House
Coltsfoot Drive
Peterborough
PE2 9BF
(01733) 890066 / 898110
info@youngwriters.co.uk